THE COMPLETE
Picture Guide
— TO —
Playing
Guitar

This publication is not authorised for sale in the
United States of America and/or Canada

WISE PUBLICATIONS
London/New York/Paris/Sydney/Copenhagen/Madrid/Tokyo

Exclusive Distributors:
Music Sales Limited
8/9 Frith Street,
London W1D 3JB, England.

Music Sales Pty Limited
120 Rothschild Avenue
Rosebery, NSW 2018,
Australia.

Order No.AM971729
ISBN 0-7119-9048-4
This book © Copyright 2001 by Wise Publications

Part One written by Arthur Dick
Edited by James Sleigh
Part Two written by Joe Bennett
Edited by Sorcha Armstrong
Photographs by George Taylor
Book design by Chloë Alexander
Music Processed by Paul Ewers
Artist photographs courtesy of
London Features International

Printed in the United Kingdom by
Caligraving Limited, Thetford, Norfolk.

Your Guarantee of Quality
As publishers, we strive to produce every book to the highest
commercial standards. The music has been freshly engraved and
the book has been carefully designed to minimise awkward page
turns and to make playing from it a real pleasure. Particular care
has been given to specifying acid-free, neutral-sized paper made
from pulps which have not been elemental chlorine bleached.
This pulp is from farmed sustainable forests and was produced
with special regard for the environment. Throughout, the printing
and binding have been planned to ensure a sturdy, attractive
publication which should give years of enjoyment. If your copy
fails to meet our high standards, please inform us and we will
gladly replace it.

Music Sales' complete catalogue describes thousands of titles and
is available in full colour sections by subject, direct from
Music Sales Limited. Please state your areas of interest and send a
cheque/postal order for £1.50 for postage to: Music Sales Limited,
Newmarket Road, Bury St. Edmunds, Suffolk IP33 3YB.

www.musicsales.com

Contents

THE COMPLETE
Picture Guide
TO
Playing
Guitar
PART ONE

By Arthur Dick

Introduction

So you have your first guitar, you've taken it out of the case, and you want to play your first chords – this book will help you learn the most commonly used guitar chords. By the end of Part One you will be able to play four famous songs by some of the world's greatest recording artists – including The Beatles and Chuck Berry.

You don't even need to be able to read music – all you have to do is copy the chord shapes a finger at a time. At every stage chord shapes and hand positions are indicated clearly with diagrams and photographs – simply look and learn!

Steel string acoustic   **Nylon string acoustic**

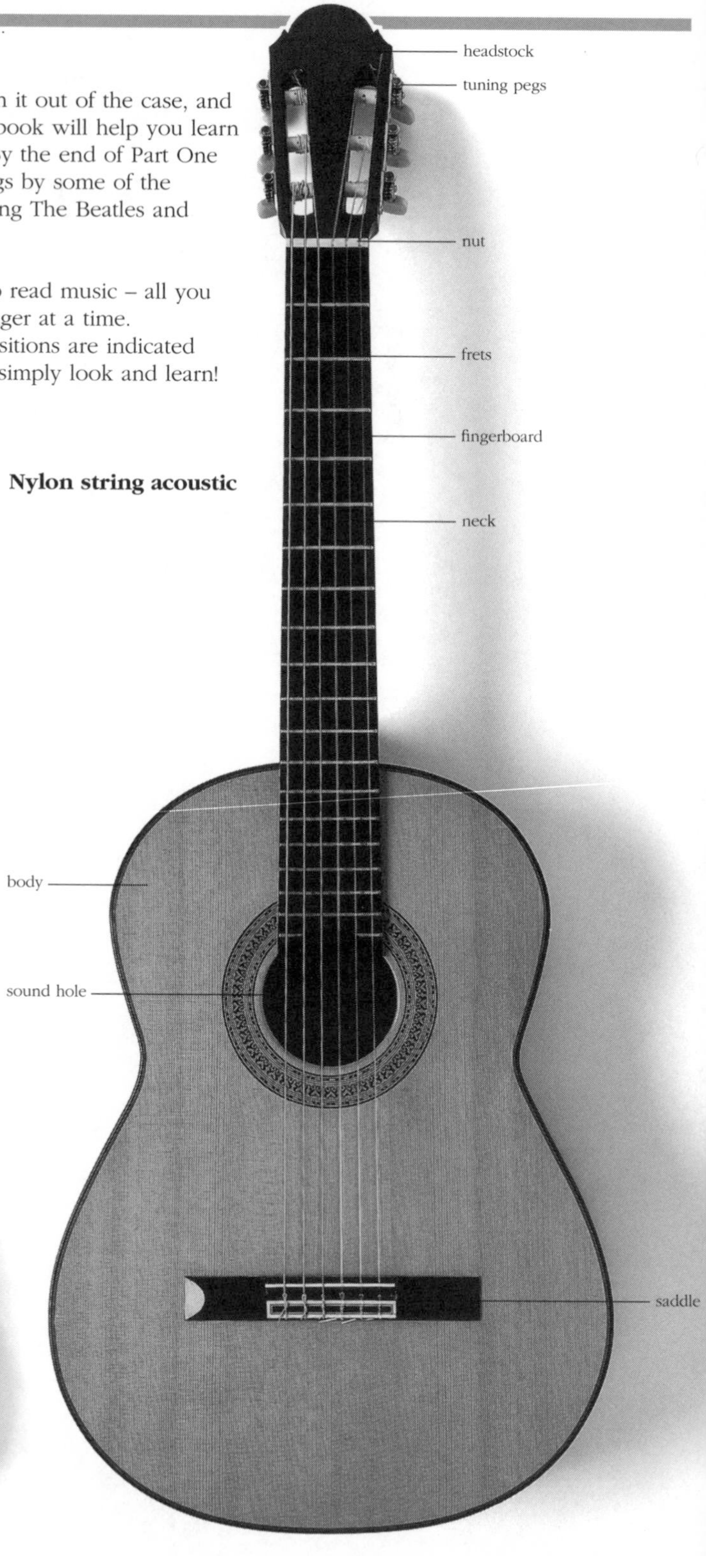

headstock

tuning pegs

nut

frets

fingerboard

neck

body

sound hole

saddle

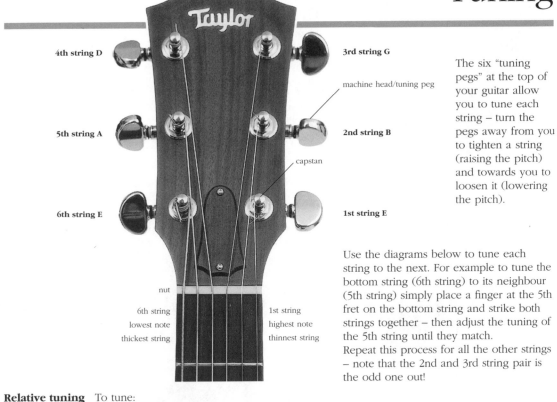

4th string D

5th string A

6th string E

3rd string G

machine head/tuning peg

2nd string B

capstan

1st string E

nut

6th string
lowest note
thickest string

1st string
highest note
thinnest string

The six "tuning pegs" at the top of your guitar allow you to tune each string – turn the pegs away from you to tighten a string (raising the pitch) and towards you to loosen it (lowering the pitch).

Use the diagrams below to tune each string to the next. For example to tune the bottom string (6th string) to its neighbour (5th string) simply place a finger at the 5th fret on the bottom string and strike both strings together – then adjust the tuning of the 5th string until they match.
Repeat this process for all the other strings – note that the 2nd and 3rd string pair is the odd one out!

Relative tuning   To tune:

| 6th to 5th string | 5th to 4th string | 4th to 3rd string | 3rd to 2nd string | 2nd to 1st string |

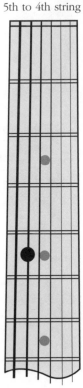

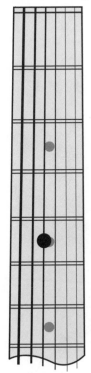

Strings and things

Wind string neatly around machinehead

Of course, there are other ways of tuning your guitar – you could use an electronic tuner, tuning pipes, or even a tuning fork. If you are playing with other people you will need to make sure your guitar is in tune with them.

Caring For The Guitar

Most guitars don't need a great deal of looking after – just make sure that you rub down the strings with a lint-free cloth before you put the guitar back in its case; this will prolong the life of the strings and prevent damage from sweaty hands!

Strings and Re-stringing

Acoustic guitars can be strung with either metal or nylon strings, but all electric guitars have metal ones. Inevitably, at some point in the life of your guitar, you will need to change the strings – either because a string has broken or because they have become dull or tarnished. Make sure you buy a replacement set of strings of the same gauge and take care as you wind the new string round the machinehead (see page 37).

Position and posture

In reality, there's no right or wrong way to hold your guitar – just check out some of the guitarists on this page to see the wide variety of postures and playing styles. The right posture is the one that feels most comfortable to you. However, for most beginners the playing positions shown below are the best – they'll prevent back pain in the long term and will make it easier to form your first chords on the fretboard.

Strumming

Before you even start to learn your first chord shapes you will need to decide whether or not to strum with a plectrum (or "pick"). The photos below give a "guitarist's-eye-view" of the two strumming styles - with pick and without. Your choice might depend on the sort of music you want to play – folk guitarists often play without a pick, whereas rock players play with one. Experiment with both methods and see which feels most natural to you.

For a beginner, a thick pick will make strumming easier – but once again, try different thicknesses and see which one feels best to you.

Rest your right arm over the body of the guitar, making sure that it is relaxed, and strum gently back and forth over the strings – the movement should be from the elbow. Don't worry about your left hand at this stage – just concentrate on creating an even, rhythmic motion across the strings.

Your left hand is probably already supporting the neck of the guitar – now move it right down to the "nut", keeping the whole arm relaxed. Playing your first chord can be a painful experience – use your thumb behind the neck to support your hand, making sure that your other fingers are not exerting too much pressure.

Relax your whole arm and
let your hand brush across
the strings as it falls.

Your first chord **A Major**

The first chord you're going to learn is called A major – because the major chords are so common they're generally referred to by their letter name only – so this chord is simply called "A".

Place your fingers one at a time making sure that each string sounds clearly. Check the final chord shape as shown below – make sure that your hand position looks the same as the photos.

Once you have mastered the whole shape, pick across each of the six strings, checking that they are all ringing clearly. If the top string is not sounding properly, check your left hand to make sure that you are not inadvertently catching your third finger against it.

The number in the circle tells you which left hand finger to use.

Final chord shape

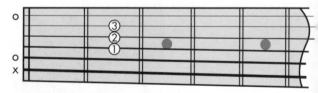

X = don't play this string   **O** = open string

Not all guitar chords use all six strings – to play this chord properly you only need to strum five of them. Although the chord of A sounds fine when all six strings are played, it sounds better if the bottom string is omitted.

This is primarily a problem for your strumming hand – practise by placing your pick (or thumb and first finger) on the fifth string and strumming from there. Gradually you will learn to target the strings you want to hit and avoid those that don't sound good.

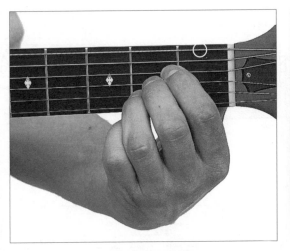

Avoid striking the bottom string

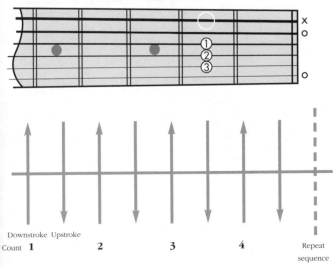

Downstroke Upstroke

Count **1**   **2**   **3**   **4**   Repeat sequence

Now practise strumming up and down rhythmically while holding down the chord of A. Try to strum up and down with a regular, even motion as you count steadily from 1 to 4 – this is what musicians refer to as the "beat". Each down strum should fall on the beat, while the up strums occur between the beats. It's vital to be able to play in time with the beat – especially if you ever want to play in a band.

A new chord **D**

Now try another major chord – this shape is known as D major or simply D. Once again this shape uses three fingers – place them one at a time on the fretboard and check that each string is sounding clearly.

Don't press down too hard with the fingers of your left hand – you'll be surprised how little pressure it actually takes to fret a chord successfully.
Positioning your thumb comfortably behind the neck can be helpful.

The number in the circle tells you which left hand finger to use.

Final chord shape

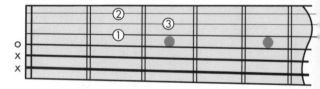

X = don't play this string   **O** = open string

This time you only need to strum the top four strings to make the chord of D – the bottom two strings should be avoided – they won't sound good!

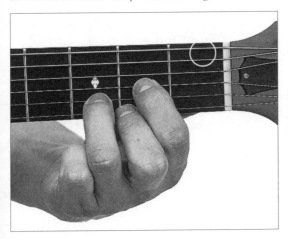

You have now learnt two of the most common chords in pop – A and D. These two chords sound great when played one after the other – you'll find this chord change in hundreds of classic songs.

Avoid striking the bottom 2 strings

Now practise A to D
You might find moving from the A shape to the D shape slightly tricky – start strumming very slowly (but rhythmically), allowing yourself plenty of time to make the change. The most important thing is to keep in time – it doesn't matter how slowly you play to start with – you can always speed up later.

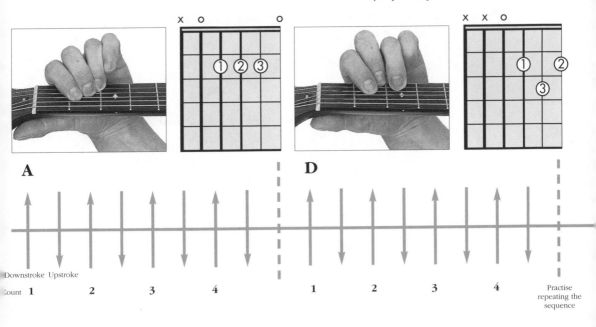

Your first song Memphis Tennessee

Armed with the chords of A and D, you're now ready to tackle a Chuck Berry classic!

This rock'n'roll tune only uses those two chords – try and make sure you change between them as smoothly as possible.

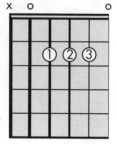

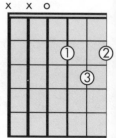

Memphis Tennessee

Words & Music by Chuck Berry

Intro | **D** | **D** | **D** | **D** ||

Verse 1

      A
Long distance information give me Memphis Tennessee,

Help me find the party tryin' to get in touch with me.
     D
She could not leave her number

But I know who placed the call
        A   **D**
'Cause my uncle took the message and he wrote it on the wall.

Verse 2

   A
Help me information get in touch with my Marie,

She's the only one who'd phone me here from Memphis Tennessee.
  D
Her home is on the south side,

High upon a ridge,
A   **D**
Just a half a mile from the Mississippi Bridge.

Instrumental | **A** | **A** | **A** | **A** |

                | **D** | **D** | **A** | **A   D** | **D** ||

Verse 3

A
Help me information, more than that I cannot add,

Only that I miss her and all the fun we had,
D
But we were pulled apart

Because her Mom did not agree
A   **D**
And tore apart our happy home in Memphis Tennessee.

Verse 4

A
The last time I saw Marie she's waving me goodbye

With hurry-home drops on her cheek that trickled from her eye,
D
Marie is only six years old,

Information please,
A   **D**
Try to put me through to her in Memphis Tennessee.

A new chord **E**

Here is possibly the most commonly used guitar chord of all time – E major. Just like A and D, the E shape uses three fingers, but this time you can safely strum all six strings.

Try and make sure your left hand fingers arch over to form a right angle with the fretboard – this will ensure that you don't catch adjacent strings. Place your fingers one at a time, following the diagrams below, then strum the final shape, making sure all six strings sound clearly.

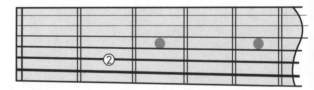

Final chord shape

X = don't play this string   **O** = open string

18

Practising **E**

Now practise changing from A to E – strum four beats of each chord, counting steadily. Try and make the transition for A to E (and back again) as smooth as possible.

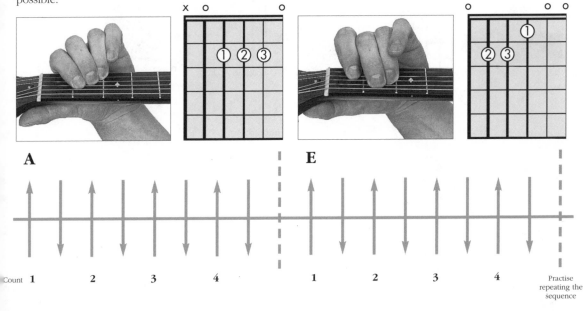

Now it's time to combine all three chords that you have learnt so far. Strum four beats of each chord, counting steadily all the time.

Try thinking ahead to the next chord shape as you strum, so that you are ready to change shape after the fourth beat.

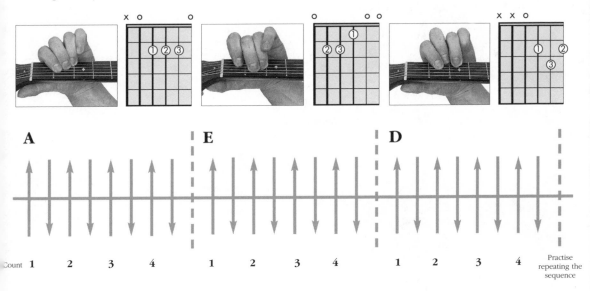

Your next song Love Me Do

The verse of the first Beatles hit single will provide you with another chance to practise changing from A to D, while the bridge section introduces the chord of E.

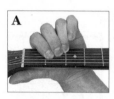

Love Me Do

Words & Music by John Lennon & Paul McCartney

Intro

| **A** | **D** | **A** | **D** | |
| **A** | **D** | **A** | **A** | ‖

Verse 1

A   **D**
Love, love me do,

  A   **D**
You know I love you,

  A   **D**
I'll always be true,

So please_____

    A **D** **A**   **D**
Love me do, oh   love me do.

Verse 2

A   **D**
Love, love me do,

  A   **D**
You know I love you,

  A   **D**
I'll always be true,

So please _____

    A **D** **A**
Love me do, oh love me do.

Bridge

E
Someone to love,

D   **A**
Somebody new,

E
Someone to love,

D   **A**
Someone like you.

Verse 3

A   **D**
Love, love me do,

  A   **D**
You know I love you,

  A   **D**
I'll always be true,

So please_____

      A D A
Love me do, oh love me do.

Instrumental ‖: **E** | **E** | **D** | **A** :‖ *Repeat this sequence*

        | **A** | **A** | **A** | **A** ‖

Verse 4

A   **D**
Love, love me do,

  A   **D**
You know I love you,

  A   **D**
I'll always be true,

So please _____

      A D A   **D**
Love me do, oh love me do.

Coda

    A
Yeah, love me do,

D **A**   **D**
Woh-oh love me do.   *(Fade)*

A new chord **C Major**

This chord is slightly more difficult than the three you have already learnt, because an open string is hidden in the middle of the chord shape.

Be careful not to catch the open third string with your second finger, and similarly, don't muffle the open top string with your first finger.

Once again, if you attempt to make your fingers meet the fingerboard at right angles you shouldn't have any problems.

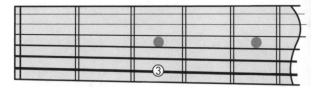

Final chord shape

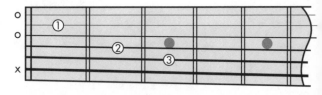

X = don't play this string   O = open string

As with the chord of A, C major will sound much better if you avoid strumming the bottom string.

Now try practising a change from C to D to A. Allow yourself plenty of time to change between the different shapes, while maintaining a steady beat.

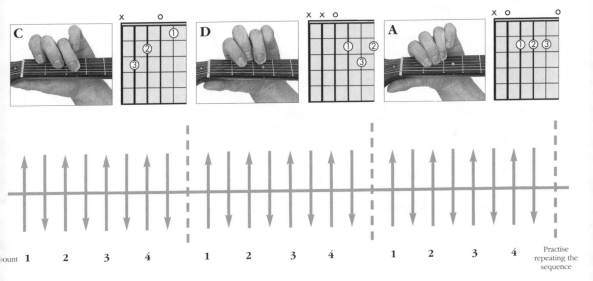

Your next song Get It On

The chords you have just been practising now come together in this T. Rex classic – Get It On.

A steady rhythmic feel is essential for this glam rocker!

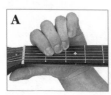

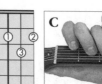

Get It On

Words & Music by Marc Bolan

Verse 1

        A
Well you're dirty and sweet,
 D   **A**
Clad in black, don't look back, and I love you,
 D   **A**
You're dirty and sweet, oh yeah.

Well you're slim and you're weak,
           D   **A**
You've got the teeth of the Hydra upon you,
 D   **A**
You're dirty sweet and you're my girl.

Chorus 1

   C   **D**   **A**
Get it on, bang a gong, get it on.
   C   **D**   **A**
Get it on, bang a gong, get it on.

Verse 2

       (A)
Well you're built like a car,
         D   **A**
You've got a hubcap diamond star halo,
 D   **A**
You're built like a car, oh yeah.

                        D
Well you're an untamed youth, that's the truth,
         A
With your cloak full of eagles
 D   **A**
You're dirty sweet and you're my girl.

Chorus 2   As Chorus 1

Verse 3

         A
Well you're windy and wild
       D   **A**
You've got the blues in your shoes and your stockings,
  D   **A**
You're windy and wild, oh yeah.

Well you're built like a car,
       D   **A**
You've got a hubcap diamond star halo,
  D   **A**
You're dirty sweet and you're my girl.

Chorus 3   As Chorus 1

Instrumental ‖: **A** | **A** | **A** | **A** :‖ *Repeat this sequence*

Verse 4

        (A)
Well you're dirty and sweet,
     D   **A**
Clad in black, don't look back, and I love you,
  D   **A**
You're dirty and sweet, oh yeah.

Well you dance when you walk,
    D   **A**
So let's dance, take a chance, understand me,
  D   **A**
You're dirty sweet and you're my girl.

Chorus 4 ‖:   **C**   **D**   **A**
           Get it on, bang a gong, get it on. :‖ *Play 3 times*

Instrumental ‖: **A** | **A** | **A** | **A** :‖

Chorus 5 ‖:   **C**   **D**   **A**
           Get it on, bang a gong, get it on. :‖ *Play 3 times*
        C   **D**   **A**
Get it on, bang a gong, right on!
        C **D** **A**
Take me!

Coda   Well meanwhile I'm still thinkin'.
(spoken)

25

A new chord **G Major**

The chord of G completes the set of five classic guitar chords that you're going to learn. G is a great-sounding open chord using all six strings.

Once again, care must be taken not to muffle the open fourth and second strings with the fretting fingers.

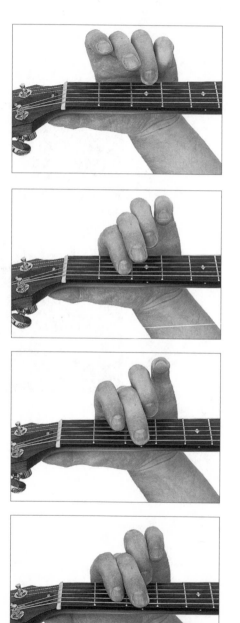

Final chord shape

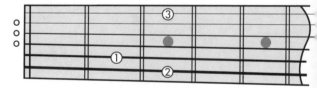

X = don't play this string   **O** = open string

26

Now practise changing from A to G.

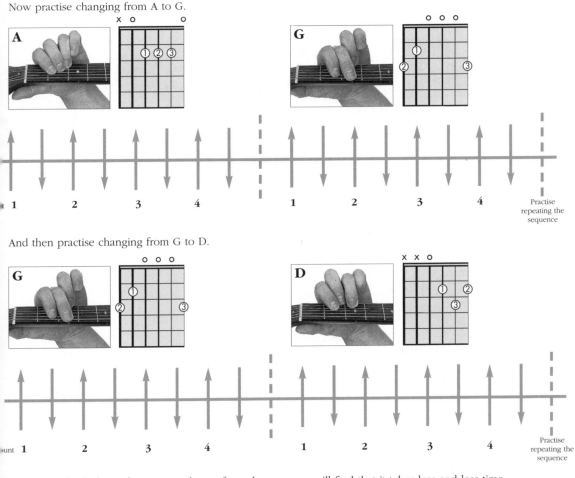

And then practise changing from G to D.

Finally, put both these changes together to form the sequence A to G to D. As you become more proficient you will find that it takes less and less time to change from one chord to the next.

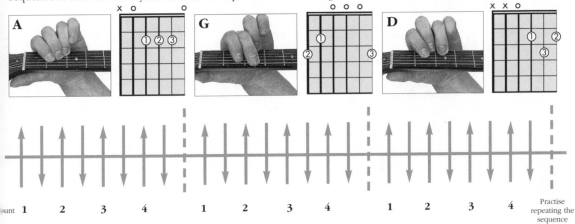

The Grand Finale Get Back

This 1969 Beatles rocker uses the chord sequence you've just been practising. Once again, the verse alternates between the chords of A and D, but look out for the fast change from G to D in the chorus!

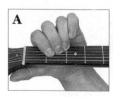

Get Back

Words & Music by John Lennon & Paul McCartney

Intro |**A** |**A** |**A** |**A** **G** **D**‖

Verse 1
A
Jo Jo was a man who thought he was a loner
D   **A**
But he knew it couldn't last.

Jo Jo left his home in Tucson, Arizona
D   **A**
For some California grass.

Chorus 1
A   **D**   **A**   **G** **D**
Get back, get back, get back to where you once belonged,
       A   **D**   **A**
Get back, get back, get back to where you once belonged.

(Get back Jo Jo).

Instrumental |**A** |**A** |**D** |**A** **G** **D**‖

Chorus 2
       A   **D**   **A**   **G** **D**
Get back, get back, get back to where you once belonged,
       A   **D**   **A**
Get back, get back, get back to where you once belonged.

(Get back Jo).

Instrumental |**A** |**A** |**D** |**A** **G** **D**‖

Verse 2
　　　　　　　A
Sweet Loretta Martin thought she was a woman
D　　　　　　　**A**
But she was another man.

All the girls around her say she's got it coming
D　　　　　　　**A**　　　**G**　**D**
But she gets it while she can.

Chorus 3　　　As Chorus 1

Instrumental　| **A**　　　| **A**　　| **D**　　| **A**　　**G**　**D** ‖

　　　　　　　A　　　　　　**D**　　　　　　　　　　　**A**　　**G**　**D**
Chorus 4　　Get back, get back, get back to where you once belonged,
　　　　　　　A　　　　　　**D**　　　　　　　　　　**A**
　　　　　　Get back, get back, get back to where you once belonged.

　　　　　　(Get back Jo).

　　　　　　　A　　　　　**D**
Coda　　　　Get back Loretta,
(spoken)　　　　　　　　**A**　　　　　　**G**　**D**
　　　　　　Your Mommy is waiting for you

　　　　　　　　　　　　　　　　　　　　　　　　　D
　　　　　　Wearin' her high-heeled shoes and her low neck sweater
　　　　　　　　　　　　　　　A　　**G**　**D**
　　　　　　Get back home Loretta.

Chorus 5　　　‖: As Chorus 1 :‖　　*Repeat to fade*

29

The Check List

Armed with the five chords you've learnt so far, you will now be able to play hundreds of classic rock tracks. Experiment with different strumming patterns and chord sequences, and maybe even try writing some songs of your own!

A

 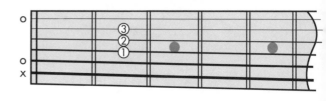

D

 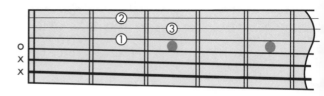

E

 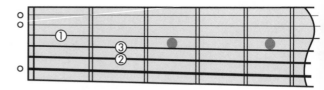

C

 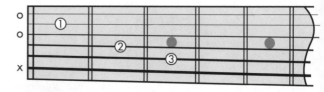

G

 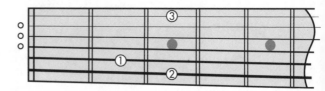

Other songs to play

Now take the five chords you've learnt and try these other classic chord sequences:

All Right Now – Free
A, D, G, E

Blue Suede Shoes – Elvis Presley
A, D, E

Born To Be Wild – Steppenwolf
A, C, D, E

Brimful Of Asha – Cornershop
A, D, E

Common People – Pulp
G, C, D

Elephant Stone – The Stone Roses
G, C, D

Hey Joe – Jimi Hendrix
C, G, D, A, E

The Jean Genie – David Bowie
A, E, D, G

Jumping Jack Flash – The Rolling Stones
Verse – **A, D, G**
Chorus – **C, G, D, A**

Lay Down Sally – Eric Clapton
A, D, E

Mr Tambourine Man – Bob Dylan
G, A, D, G, D, G, A

Paperback Writer – The Beatles
G, C, D

Peggy Sue – Buddy Holly
A, D, E

Shaker Maker – Oasis
Verse – **A, D, A, G, D, A**

Walk Of Life – Dire Straits
A, D, E

Some other chords to try out

If this introduction to the world of chords has whetted your appetite, check out some other essential chord shapes:

Remember that not all chords use all six strings - so take care which strings you hit!

Don't strike the 6th string!

A minor

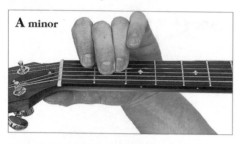

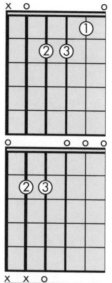

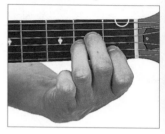

E minor

Don't strike the 5th and 6th strings!

D7

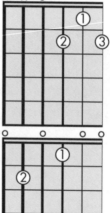

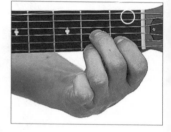

E7

Don't strike the 6th string!

A7

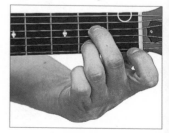

Now try these songs

These extra shapes open up new possibilities, as demonstrated by these rock standards:

Imagine – John Lennon
Verse: **G**, **C**, **G**, **C**, **G**, **C**, **G**, **C**
Chorus: **Em**, **Am**, **C**, **D**

All Along The Watchtower – Bob Dylan/Jimi Hendrix
Em,**C**, **D**

Eleanor Rigby – The Beatles
Em, **C**, **Em**, **C**

Everything Must Go – Manic Street Preachers
Chorus: **E**, **Am**, **D**, **E**

Love Is All Around – Wet Wet Wet
G, **Am**, **C**, **D**

Massachusetts – The Bee Gees
G, **Am**, **C**, **G**

Roll Over Beethoven – Chuck Berry
A7, **D7**, **E7**

Lady Jane – The Rolling Stones
C, **G**, **D**, **E**, **Am**, **D7**

You now know enough to play all these great songs from The Picture Guide To Playing Guitar Songbook 1:

All Along The Watchtower Jimi Hendrix

All Right Now Free

Born To Be

Wild Steppenwolf

Dedicated Follower Of Fashion The Kinks

Hey Jude The Beatles

Imagine John Lennon

Johnny B. Goode Chuck Berry

Knockin' On Heaven's Door Bob Dylan

Lay Down Sally Eric Clapton

Love Is All Around Wet Wet Wet

Mrs. Robinson Simon & Garfunkel

Roll Over Beethoven Chuck Berry

Walk Of Life Dire Straits

Wonderful Tonight Eric Clapton

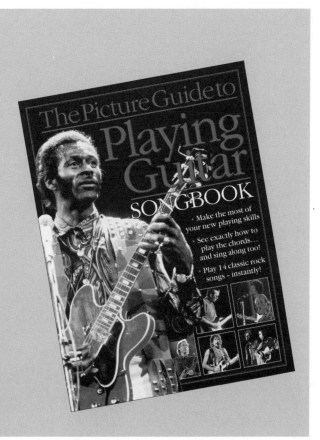

The Picture Guide to Playing Guitar SONGBOOK

- Make the most of your new playing skills
- See exactly how to play the chords... and sing along too!
- Play 14 classic rock songs - instantly!

THE COMPLETE

Picture Guide

TO

Playing
Guitar

PART TWO

By Joe Bennett

Introduction

Congratulations on completing Part One of The Complete Picture Guide To Playing Guitar. Like many millions of guitarists around the world, you now know the chords A, D, E, C and G. Having got this far, you can probably play at least half a dozen songs already, and want to take your playing to the next level.

In Part One, you learned five chords and some basic strumming techniques, along with four songs to play.

In Part Two, we're going to introduce four new chords, learn some more advanced strumming techniques, and discover the art of playing lead guitar.

We're also going to look at some classic songs in detail – Jimi Hendrix's *Hey Joe*, Don McLean's *American Pie*, and John Lennon's *Imagine*, plus lead parts for songs by The Beatles, Ocean Colour Scene and Elvis Presley.

Guitar Gear

Strings
Packaged as singles or sets of six. There are three main types – one for each type of guitar.

Plectrum
Also known as a 'pick'. These come in various thicknesses, and are usually made of plastic. Start with a medium one.

Capo
A snap-on device which fits over the frets, raising the guitar's pitch and making it possible to play in different keys.

Amplifier or 'Combo'
Electric guitars need amplification as they don't create much sound by themselves. Plug it in and turn up the volume!

Bottleneck
Also known as a slide. Used on electric and acoustic steel-strings, usually for Blues or Hawaiian music.

Electronic Tuner
Works on any type of guitar. A quick way of getting your guitar accurately in tune.

How to change strings

You should aim to change all of your guitar's strings at least once a year. Some professional players change theirs every few hours!

When you change strings, change the whole set at the same time – this will ensure you don't get an uneven sound out of your guitar.

Acoustic and electric guitars

1 Remove one string from the guitar by loosening the tuning peg completely.

2 Thread the new string through the bridge. Some acoustic guitars have a peg to keep each string in place.

3 Thread the other end through the capstan by the tuning peg, leaving around 2 cm of slack.

4 Turn the peg until the string is tight, then check the tuning. Cut off the unused extra length using wire cutters.

Nylon-strung guitars

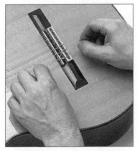

1 Remove one string from the guitar by loosening the tuning peg completely. You will need to untie the string at the bridge end.

2 Thread the string through the bridge, then twist the string around itself a few times. The taut string will eventually keep your twists in place.

3 Thread the other end through the capstan, leaving around 2 cm protruding at the end.

4 Wind all the rest of the string onto the capstan – this may take lots of turns of the peg – and tune to the correct pitch.

Hey Joe

Jimi Hendrix

Using the five chords you learned in Part One, you can now play a rhythm guitar part for this Jimi Hendrix classic.

Use two strong down-strums for every chord change, adding upstrokes in between if you feel confident enough.

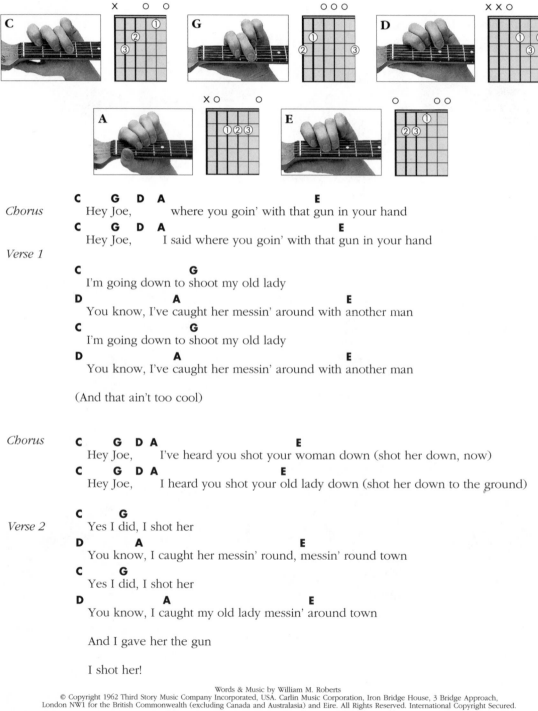

Chorus

```
C   G   D   A                              E
Hey Joe,        where you goin' with that gun in your hand
C    G   D   A                               E
Hey Joe,        I said where you goin' with that gun in your hand
```

Verse 1

```
C                    G
I'm going down to shoot my old lady
D               A                        E
You know, I've caught her messin' around with another man
C                    G
I'm going down to shoot my old lady
D               A                          E
You know, I've caught her messin' around with another man
```

(And that ain't too cool)

Chorus

```
C    G  D A                         E
Hey Joe,      I've heard you shot your woman down (shot her down, now)
C    G  D A                  E
Hey Joe,      I heard you shot your old lady down (shot her down to the ground)
```

Verse 2

```
C    G
Yes I did, I shot her
D        A                        E
You know, I caught her messin' round, messin' round town
C    G
Yes I did, I shot her
D          A                      E
You know, I caught my old lady messin' around town
```

And I gave her the gun

I shot her!

Words & Music by William M. Roberts
© Copyright 1962 Third Story Music Company Incorporated, USA. Carlin Music Corporation, Iron Bridge House, 3 Bridge Approach, London NW1 for the British Commonwealth (excluding Canada and Australasia) and Eire. All Rights Reserved. International Copyright Secured.

Solo | **C G** | **D A** | **E** | **E** | *x2*

Riff | **C G** | **D A** | **E** | **E** |
see page 28

         C   **G**   **D A**   **E**
Chorus   Hey Joe (said now)   where you gonna run to now? (where you gonna run to?)
         C   **G**   **D A**   **E**
            Hey Joe, (I said)   where you gonna run to now? (where you, where you gonna go?)

         (Well, dig it)

         C   **G**   **D A**
Verse 3   I'm goin' way down south,
                           E
         Way down to Mexico way (alright)
         C   **G**   **D A**
            I'm goin' way down south,
                           E
         Way down where I can be free (ain't no one gonna find me)

         C   **G**   **D**
Coda   Ain't no hangman gonna,
         A   **E**
         He ain't gonna put a rope around me (you better believe it right now)

         (*ad lib to fade*)

Jimi Hendrix

New chords **Am** and **Em**

In this section, we're going to look at two new chords. These are called **minor chords** and they can help to add a darker, more interesting sound than the five **major chords** you've learned so far.

In chord sheets, minor chords have the same letter names as other chords, but include the abbreviation 'm' after their letter name.

How to play Am and Em
Place your fingers one at a time, following the diagrams to the left and below, then strum the final shape, making sure all the strings sound clearly. Try to make sure your left hand fingers arch over the fretboard, so you don't catch adjacent strings. The Am chord is to the left, and the Em chord is below.

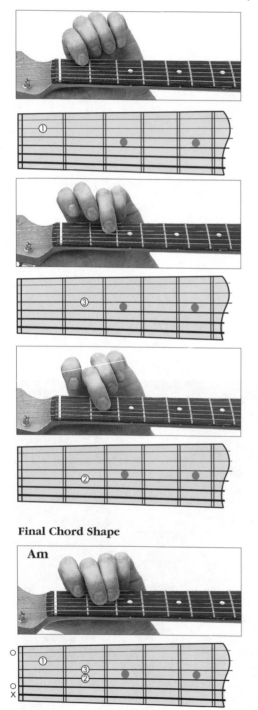

Final Chord Shape

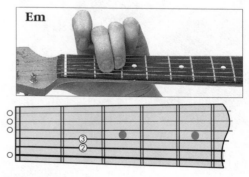

Final Chord Shape

Practising **Am** and **Em**

Now, practise changing from Am to Em – starting with a downstroke, strum four beats of each chord, counting steadily. Note that the fingering for Em, which might at first seem difficult, actually helps to make the change between chords easier. Once you can play even down and upstrokes whilst changing chords without a pause, you're ready to tackle the chord sequence for *American Pie* over the page.

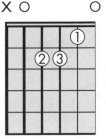

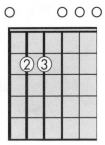

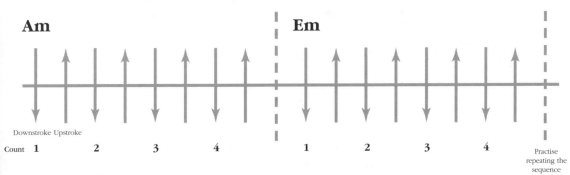

Am

Downstroke Upstroke

Count **1**   **2**   **3**   **4**

Em

1   **2**   **3**   **4**

Practise
repeating the
sequence

Strumming Tips

- Use a slightly thicker pick to make strumming easier.
- Make sure that your right arm is relaxed, and resting over the body of the guitar (see picture).
- The strumming movement should come from your elbow and not your wrist.
- Try to concentrate on creating an even, rhythmic motion across the strings.

Be careful not to hit the sixth (thickest) string when you strum the A minor chord.

American Pie

Don McLean

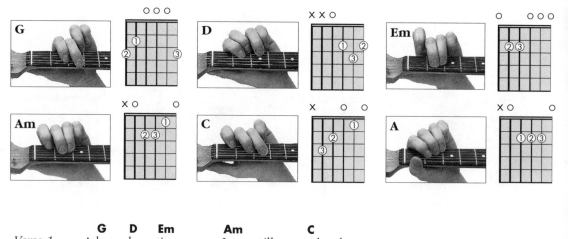

Verse 1

    G   **D**   **Em**   **Am**   **C**
A long, long time ago… I can still remember how
     Em   **D**
That music used to make me smile.
    G   **D**   **Em**   **Am**   **C**
And I knew if I had my chance, that I could make those people dance,
     Em   **C**   **D**
And maybe they'd be happy for a while.
Em   **Am**   **Em**   **Am**
But February made me shiver, with every paper I'd deliver,
C   **G**   **Am**   **C**   **D**
Bad news on the doorstep… I couldn't take one more step.
    G   **D**   **Em**   **C**   **D**
I can't remember if I cried when I read about his widowed bride
    G   **D**   **Em**   **C**   **D**   **G**
But something touched me deep inside, the day the music died.

Chorus 1

     G **C**   **G**   **D**
So bye, bye Miss American Pie
            G   **C**   **G**   **D**
Drove my Chevy to the levee but the levee was dry
     G   **C**   **G**   **D**
Them good ol' boys were drinking whisky and rye
        Em   **A**
Singing this'll be the day that I die
Em   **D**
This'll be the day that I die

Words & Music by Don McLean
© Copyright 1971 Music Corporation Of America Incorporated & Benny Bird Company Incorporated, USA. Universal/MCA Music Limited,
77 Fulham Palace Road, London W6. All Rights Reserved. International Copyright Secured.

Verse 2

```
      G                  Am              C              Am
   Did you write the book of love and do you have faith in God above
   Em        D
   If the Bible tells you so
      G    D    Em          Am            C
   And do you believe in rock and roll, can music save your mortal soul
      Em           A        D
   And can you teach me how to dance real slow?
      Em              D                    Em              D
   Well I know that you're in love with him 'cause I saw you dancing in the gym
      C              Am      C              D
   You both kicked off your shoes man I dig those rhythm and blues
      G    D    Em              Am              C
   I was a lonely teenage broncin' buck with a pink carnation and a pick up truck
      G    D    Em          C      D         G  C  G
   But I knew I was out of luck the day the music died
      D
   I started singin'…
```

(repeat chorus)

Verse 3
Now for 10 years we've been on our own
And moss grows fat on a rolling stone
But that's not how it used to be
When the jester sang for the king and queen
In a coat he borrowed from James Dean
In a voice that came from you and me
And while the King was looking down
The jester stole his thorny crown
The court room was adjourned
No verdict was returned

And while Lennon read a book on Marx
The quartet practised in the park
And we sang dirges in the dark
The day the music died
We were singin'…

(repeat chorus)

Verse 4
Helter Skelter in a summer swelter
The Byrds flew off with a fallout shelter
Eight miles high and falling fast
It landed foul on the grass
The players tried for a forward pass
With the jester on the sidelines in a cast
Now the halftime air was sweet perfume
While sergeants played a marching tune
We all got up to dance
Oh, but we never got the chance

'Cause the players tried to take the field,
The marching band refused to yield.
Do you recall what was revealed
The day the music died?
We started singing…

(repeat chorus)

Verse 5
Oh and there we were all in one place
A generation lost in space
With no time left to start again
So come on Jack be nimble, Jack be quick
Jack Flash sat on a candlestick
'Cause fire is the Devil's only friend.
As I watched him on the stage
My hands were clenched in fists of rage
No angel born in hell
Could break that Satan's spell

And as the flames climbed high into the night
To light the sacrificial rite
I saw Satan laughing with delight
The day the music died.
He was singing…

(repeat chorus)

Verse 6
I met a girl who sang the blues
And I asked her for some happy news
But she just smiled and turned away
I went down to the sacred store
Where I'd heard the music years before
But the man there said the music wouldn't play
And in the streets the children screamed
The lovers cried and the poets dreamed
But not a word was spoken
The church bells all were broken

And the three men I admire most
The Father Son and Holy Ghost
They caught the last train for the coast
The day the music died
And they were singing…

(repeat chorus x2)
```
              C              D        G  C  G
   Singing this will be the day that I die
```

43

A new chord **F**

This is the most challenging chord you've learned so far, because it features a technique called a **partial barre**. This means you have to fret two strings with one finger. This is difficult (and painful!) at first,

so practise the chord over and over until all four notes ring out clearly. Remember not to strum those two bass strings.

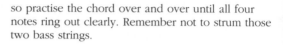

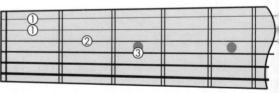

Final Chord Shape

A new chord **Dm**

The next chord you're going to learn looks a lot like the D chord you already know, but take a closer look and you'll see that the fingering is completely different. This is a four-string chord, so be sure to avoid strumming the two bass strings.

Practising F and Dm

Try this short chord sequence (taken from John Lennon's 'Imagine') using simple down-strums. It uses the chord of A minor along with both of the new shapes on this page. This is your first example of a half-bar change, meaning that some of the chords last for only two down-strums rather than four. This gives you less thinking time to change, so be sure to try the exercise at a slower tempo and build up the speed gradually. Once you've perfected this exercise, you're ready to try the full version of *Imagine* over the page.

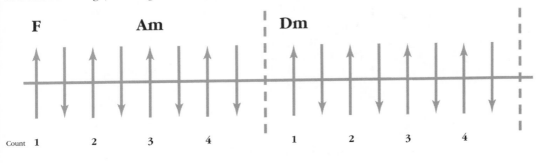

Imagine

John Lennon

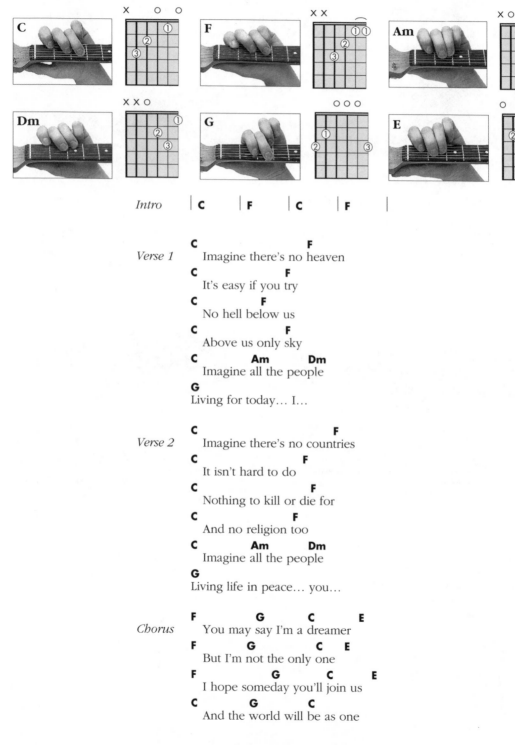

Intro | C | F | C | F |

Verse 1

C   F
Imagine there's no heaven
C   F
It's easy if you try
C   F
No hell below us
C   F
Above us only sky
C   Am   Dm
Imagine all the people
G
Living for today... I...

Verse 2

C   F
Imagine there's no countries
C   F
It isn't hard to do
C   F
Nothing to kill or die for
C   F
And no religion too
C   Am   Dm
Imagine all the people
G
Living life in peace... you...

Chorus

F   G   C   E
You may say I'm a dreamer
F   G   C E
But I'm not the only one
F   G   C   E
I hope someday you'll join us
C   G   C
And the world will be as one

<pre>
              C   F
Verse 3   Imagine no possessions
              C   F
            I wonder if you can
              C   F
            No need for greed or hunger
              C   F
            A brotherhood of man
              F   Am   Dm
            Imagine all the people
              G
            Sharing all the world…

              F   G   C   E
Chorus   You may say I'm a dreamer
              F   G   C   E
            But I'm not the only one
              F   G   C   E
            I hope someday you'll join us
              F   G   C
            And the world will live as one
</pre>

John Lennon

47

How to read guitar music

Guitarists often use a form of music notation called tablature, or TAB for short. It's a simplified version of the fingerboard pictures we've already seen (e.g. page 40) – six horizontal lines represent the strings, with the thickest string at the bottom of the diagram.

The numbers in tablature represent the fret number (so, for example, a 3 would mean press the string at the third fret). A zero in tablature means you should pluck the open string. Unlike fingerboard diagrams, tab doesn't tell us which finger to use, but it makes up for this by cramming a lot of music into a very small space. Tab can be used to show chords or single notes.

Pluck the first string 'open', i.e. without fretting a note...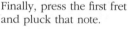

Now press the third fret on the second string and pluck that note...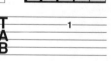

 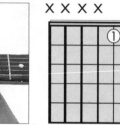

Finally, press the first fret and pluck that note.

'Three Blind Mice'

All of the above information can be shown in tab like this.

Using tab for chords

To notate chords, we simply stack the tab numbers on top of each other to show that all the notes are strummed at the same time. Here's a chord of Em shown in tab.

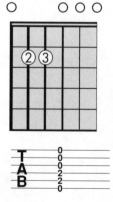 

TAB Chords

To show how easy tab is to use, here's a version of
every chord you've learned so far, with the tablature
shown under the photo.

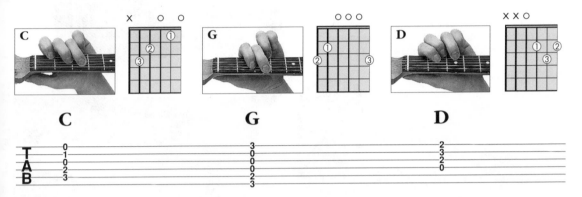

C   G   D

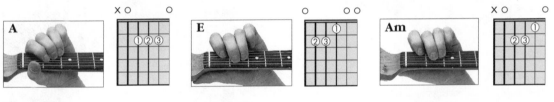

A   E   Am

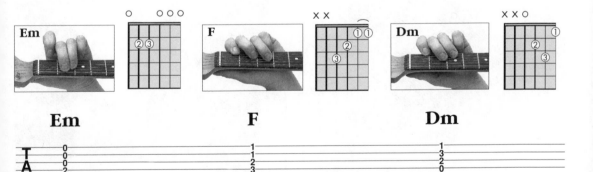

Em   F   Dm

Playing lead guitar

Now you've tried playing the chords to some famous songs, it's time to try out some lead guitar parts. Lead guitar simply means playing one note at a time, and it can apply to electric or acoustic guitar. Although lots of famous players have used their fingers or thumb to play lead (Mark Knopfler of Dire Straits, or 1960s jazzer Wes Montgomery), most beginners find it easier to start with a plectrum.

Tips for better lead playing

Don't hold the plectrum too firmly or you'll be too tense to pluck the strings accurately

Keep the plectrum close to the strings, even when you're not playing a note

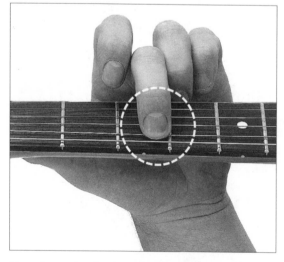

If you're getting fret buzz from a note, move your fretting hand closer to the next fret to clean up the sound.

It may help accuracy if you anchor your hand somewhere on the body. Many players like to rest on their little finger, like this.

A long strap may look cool, but it makes lead playing a lot more difficult.

Pick near to the soundhole for a well-rounded tone. If you're playing electric, pick just past the end of the neck, over the pickup.

A good lead player uses a combination of up and downstrokes to aid speed.

Make sure your fretting hand has short fingernails – this will make fretted notes easier to hold.

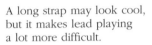

Learning the notes

On these two pages, you'll see photos, diagrams and tablature for the 8 notes you'll need to play the lead guitar parts for *Love Me Tender* and *Theme from*

Eastenders. Four of these are open notes – the fretting hand isn't used.

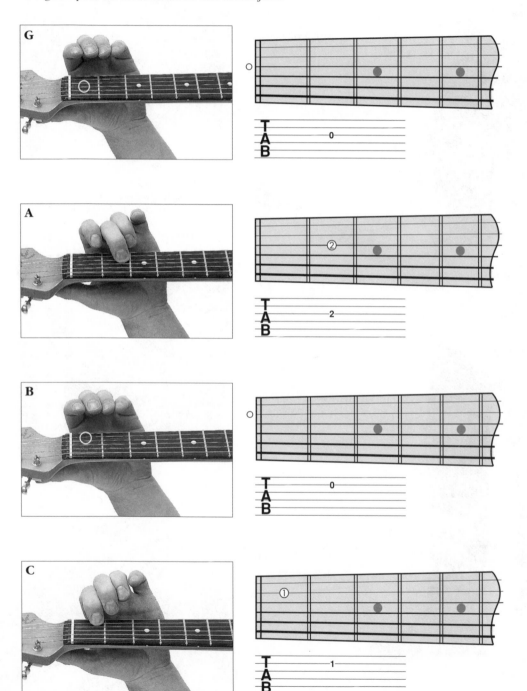

D

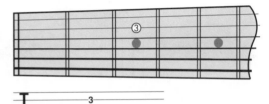

E

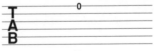

F

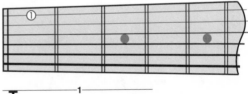

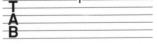

D

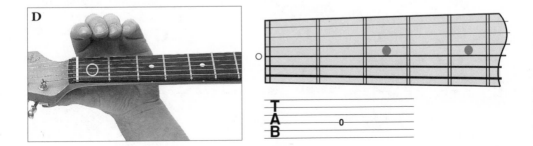

Love Me Tender

Elvis Presley

The melody for this Elvis Presley standard is actually from an American folk tune, called 'Aura Lee'. Here's the song notated in tab, with the chord names written above.

You can play the song on rhythm or lead guitar, or better still get a friend to play the chords while you take the lead part – your first duet!

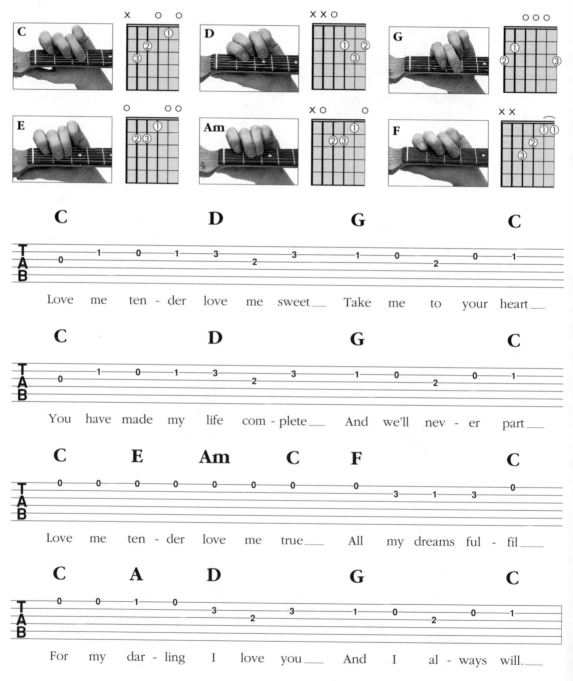

Love me ten - der love me sweet__ Take me to your heart__

You have made my life com - plete__ And we'll nev - er part__

Love me ten - der love me true__ All my dreams ful - fil__

For my dar - ling I love you__ And I al - ways will.__

Words & Music by Elvis Presley & Vera Matson

Theme from Eastenders

This is the UK's most famous piece of music. It's also a great tune for developing your lead playing, as it introduces the idea of *scalic* lines i.e. a melody where the notes are next to each other in the musical scale. As with all lead parts, you'll get the best results if you start slowly and build up to full speed.

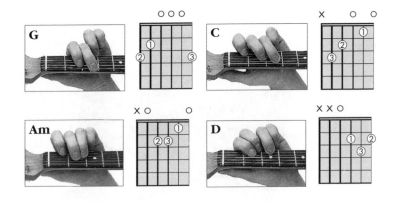

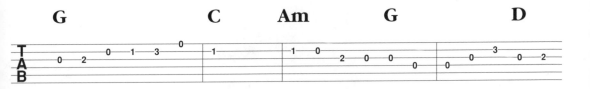

By Leslie Osborne & Simon May
© Copyright 1985 ATV Music. Sony/ATV Music Publishing (UK) Limited, 10 Great Marlborough Street, London W1.

Your first riffs

A riff is a short musical phrase, almost always played on lead guitar, which is repeated over and over at various points in the song. It forms the musical 'hook' that makes the listener remember the track. Riffs are one, two, or four bars in length, and the best ones are usually the simplest. Think of the Rolling Stones' *Satisfaction*, Nirvana's *Smells Like Teen Spirit* or Jimi Hendrix's *Purple Haze* – the songs wouldn't be half as good without that repeating guitar line.

Famous riffs

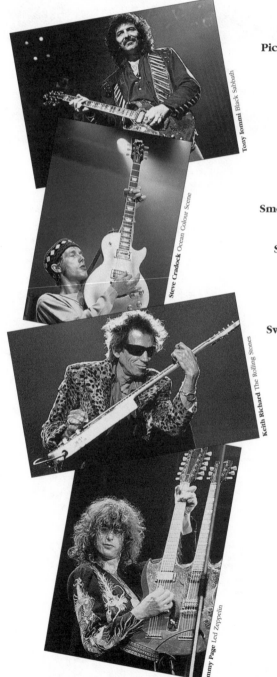

Tony Iommi Black Sabbath

Steve Cradock Ocean Colour Scene

Keith Richard The Rolling Stones

Jimmy Page Led Zeppelin

All Right Now
Free

Another One Bites The Dust
Queen

Baker Street
Gerry Rafferty

Black Night
Deep Purple

Cars
Gary Numan

Day Tripper
The Beatles

Design For Life
Manic Street Preachers

Enter Sandman
Metallica

Layla
Eric Clapton

Livin' on a Prayer
Bon Jovi

Paranoid
Black Sabbath

Parisienne Walkways
Gary Moore

Parklife
Blur

Pick A Part That's New
Stereophonics

River Boat Song
Ocean Colour Scene

Rock 'n' Roll
Led Zeppelin

Satisfaction
The Rolling Stones

Smells Like Teen Spirit
Nirvana

Smoke on the Water
Deep Purple

Stayin' Alive
The Bee Gees

Sweet Home Alabama
Lynyrd Skynyrd

The Last Time
The Rolling Stones

Ticket to Ride
The Beatles

Voodoo Chile
Jimi Hendrix

Walk This Way
Aerosmith

Whole Lotta Love
Led Zeppelin

Ticket To Ride riff

This simple 1-bar Beatles riff is based on a chord of A, and involves holding down the whole chord, then lifting off the third finger just in time to play the open note at the end of the riff. The riff can be played over and over in a continuous loop.

Hold down that A chord – it features four of the five notes in the riff.

A

The Beatles

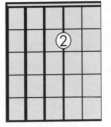

The starting note of A

A new note – C♯ at the second fret.

The Riff

Here's the riff notated in tab, below. Hold down the A chord, and then when you get to the open B note, take off your third finger, and strum the open note. Then put it back again to repeat the riff. Easy!

A

DayTripper riff

The Beatles

This riff, taken from another Beatles classic, is considerably more difficult because you need to pick each note separately and accurately at quite a speed. You may find it easier if you use all downstrokes with the plectrum at first, because the co-ordination between picking hand and fretting hand is quite a challenge!

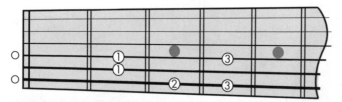

E

Day Tripper – **suggested fingering for the notes**

George Harrison

Ocean Colour Scene

The Riverboat Song riff

Although this 1990s riff is only based on three notes, it's the first time we've gone beyond the safe area of the first three frets, and it also features your first 'closed position' (i.e. it doesn't use any open notes). Don't panic! Most guitars have a dot marker at the seventh fret to help the player to find the right position quickly (and even if your guitar doesn't have them, you could always stick bits of paper on the side of the neck).

The song uses 'position playing' – meaning that you should keep your hand in one place all the time and use different fingers to fret the notes. This is the key to fast, accurate lead playing.

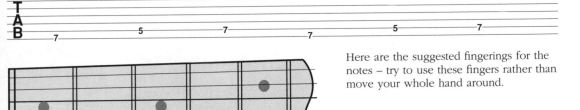

Here are the suggested fingerings for the notes – try to use these fingers rather than move your whole hand around.

Steve Cradock

Words & Music by Simon Fowler, Steve Cradock, Oscar Harrison & Damon Minchella

59

The Finale – The **Hey Joe** riff   Jimi Hendrix

Now that you can play *Hey Joe* as a rhythm guitar part (see page 38), let's try to incorporate this famous riff into the song. Jimi Hendrix played this lead part together with bass player Noel Redding – it appears at the end of the guitar solo, just before the final vocal section.

You will need to use the 'one-finger-per-fret' technique as much as possible in order to achieve the speed. The rhythm guitar part's chords of C, G, D, A and E are written above. Good luck!

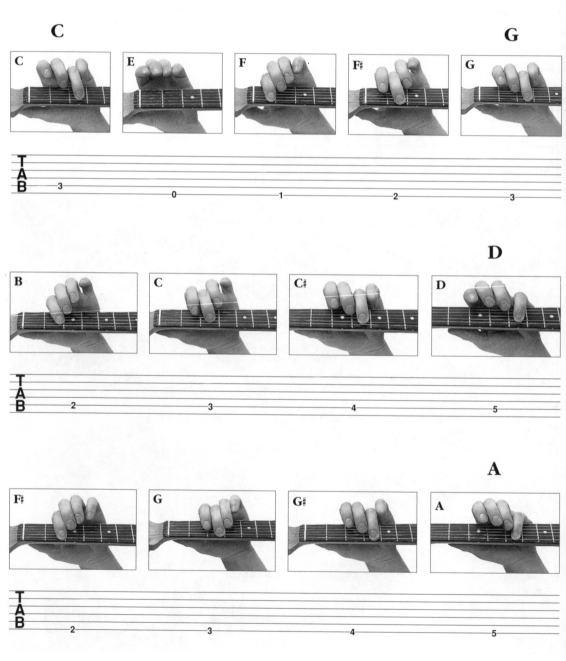

E

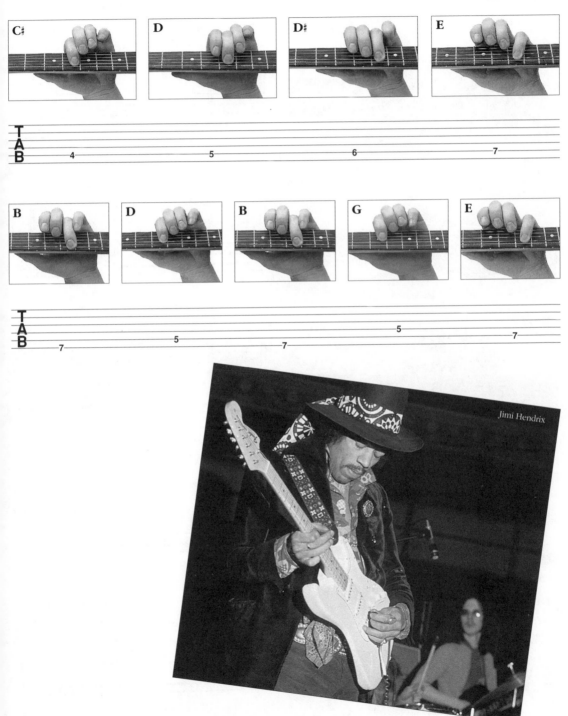

C#　　D　　D#　　E

```
T
A
B ──4──────5──────6──────7──
```

B　　D　　B　　G　　E

```
T                    5        7
A
B ─7────5────7────────────────
```

Jimi Hendrix

Some other chords to try out

You now know a total of 12 chords. Here are some more well-loved guitar chord shapes to try.

Some of these have a more jazzy, interesting sound than straight major or minor chords.

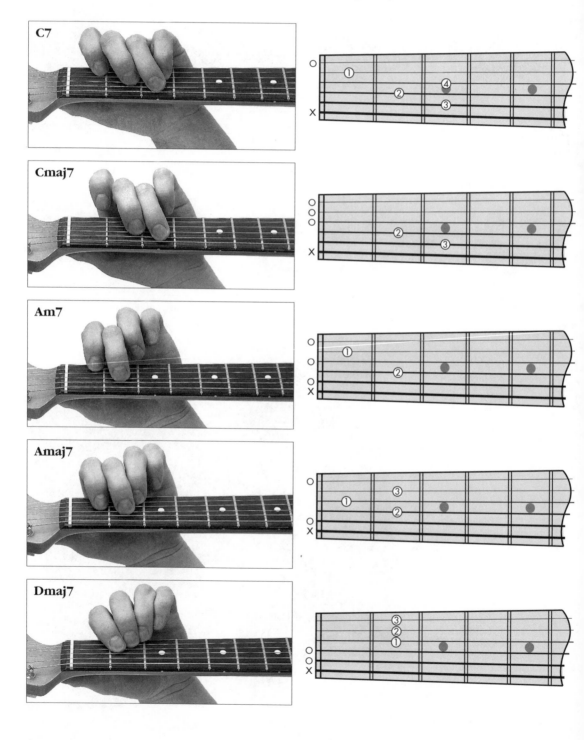

C7

Cmaj7

Am7

Amaj7

Dmaj7

On this page I've included some of the questions that guitar teachers get asked most often. These general guidelines should make your next steps into the world of the guitar a little easier.

Q I've got really big (or small) hands, so it's more difficult for me to cope with the chords.

A The guitar neck is designed to be suitable for all hand sizes. It may seem that those chord stretches are impossible at first, and that your fingers are falling over each other, but this is down to co-ordination rather than physical build. Persevere and your fingers will learn the shapes.

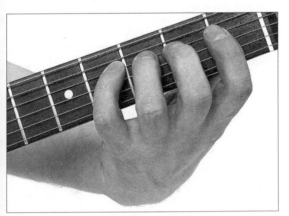

Q I've tuned up my guitar using the instructions on page 7, but when I play with another guitarist it still sounds wrong. Why?

A A guitar can be in tune with itself and yet out of tune with another guitar. Try tuning both guitars to a common reference point such as a piano or an electronic tuner.

Q Why do I find it more difficult to strum with a plectrum than with fingers?

A Either you're holding the plectrum too firmly, or your plectrum is a very thick, tough one. Try a thinner plectrum and a lighter touch.

Q How should I clean my guitar?

A Any soft cloth will do the job. An occasional rub with furniture polish is OK too as long as your guitar is lacquered or varnished to begin with. Wipe the strings before and after you play, and wash your hands every time – this will prolong string life.

Further Reading

Congratulations! You've successfully completed The Complete Guide To Playing Guitar method. Why not check out some of these other exciting titles by Joe Bennett, available from all good music retailers and book shops, or in case of difficulty, directly from Music Sales (see page 2 for details).

Really Easy Guitar!
Now you can play along with your favourite bands! Each book in this series for beginners gives you chords and lyrics for 14 great songs, and tips on how to play those famous riffs, plus a full-length 'soundalike' backing track on CD for each song.

Really Easy Guitar! Rock Classics

AM957693
Includes 'All Along The Watchtower', 'All Right Now', 'Livin' On A Prayer', ' Sultans Of Swing' and 'Wonderwall'.

Really Easy Guitar! Eric Clapton
AM968462
Includes 'Sunshine Of Your Love', 'White Room', 'Layla', 'Wonderful Tonight' and 'Tears In Heaven'.

Really Easy Guitar! The Beatles
NO90692
Includes 'And I Love Her', 'Day Tripper', 'Get Back', 'Ticket To Ride', 'Yesterday' and 'Lucy In The Sky With Diamonds'.

Really Easy Guitar! '90s Hits
AM957715
Includes 'Animal Nitrate', 'Disco 2000', 'Nothing Else Matters', 'Parklife', 'Supersonic' and 'Wild Wood'.

Guitar On Tap!
AM962214
Looking for a fancy chord? Want to play with an alternative tuning or learn a cool new riff? Or just want to brush up on your scales? It's all in Guitar On Tap! This book has been specially designed to put all the most common information guitar players need in just one book, using clear diagrams and photos.

It's Easy To Bluff...

Become an instant expert and amaze your friends! Each book includes player/ band biographies, a history of the guitar style, musical examples and lots of handy tips and tricks to help you 'bluff your way through' any situation! The Music Theory book contains composer biogs, a history of classical and popular music, all the theory you'll ever need, plus a section on musical instruments. Show them what you've got – it's Easy To Bluff!

It's Easy To Bluff... Blues Guitar
AM955196
It's Easy To Bluff... Rock Guitar
AM955218
It's Easy To Bluff... Metal Guitar
AM955207
It's Easy To Bluff... Acoustic Guitar
AM955174
It's Easy To Bluff... Jazz Guitar
AM955185
It's Easy To Bluff... Music Theory
AM958485

The Picture Guide To Playing Guitar Songbook

AM963864
14 classic rock songs for you to play, using just the chords you learnt in this book. Includes: 'All Right Now', 'Johnny B.Goode', 'Love Is All Around' and 'Wonderful Tonight'.

11/01 (41884)